Transformational Gratitude Journal

@transformationaljournals

THESE EXPRESSIONS OF GRATITUDE BELONG TO:

_____
_____
_____

Gratitude Journal Guide

✿ ✿ ✿ ✿ ✿ ✿ ✿ ✿ ✿ ✿

This gratitude journal has the power to help you transform your life in a positive way. Get into the habit of recording things and experiences for which you are grateful. Keep this journal by your bedside and determine when the best time of day is for you; before you go to sleep at nights or when you arise in the mornings.

Write about at least five positive things or experiences every day for which you are grateful. Recording positive things you are thankful for in your life will make you a happier person. Feeling and expressing gratitude for even the small things that you have, or that happens to you, can improve physical, emotional and social well-being. What you are grateful for can be as simple as "family" or as deep as "the sunset in the evening during your evening walk".

Write about something you appreciate about yourself each day. Take time to acknowledge the positives you have done for you and others. This will help to recognize how valuable you are to yourself and the world. See the good you do each day and celebrate you. Appreciating who you are each day helps you to grow to love yourself unconditionally; transforming you into a happier and more positive person.

Gratitude means "the feeling of being thankful; readiness to show appreciation for and to return kindness" The gratitude quotes are included to inspire, uplift and help you find happiness in your everyday life. These gratitude quotes serves as a boost to remind yourself that you have so much to be thankful for- each and every day!

The blank pages at the end are for you to reflect and write notes on how being grateful daily has transformed your life.

❁❁❁❁❁

Start each day with a positive thought and a grateful heart.

-*Roy T. Bennett*

MY HEART IS FILLED WITH GRATITUDE
❀❀❀❀❀

DATE:

I AM GRATEFUL FOR.....
1. _____
2. _____
3. _____
4. _____
5. _____

WHAT DO I APPRECIATE ABOUT MYSELF?
_____

DATE:

I AM GRATEFUL FOR.....
1. _____
2. _____
3. _____
4. _____
5. _____

WHAT DO I APPRECIATE ABOUT MYSELF?
_____

If you want to turn your life around, try thankfulness. It will change your life mightily.

—Gerald Good

MY HEART IS FILLED WITH GRATITUDE

DATE:

I AM GRATEFUL FOR.....

1. _____
2. _____
3. _____
4. _____
5. _____

WHAT DO I APPRECIATE ABOUT MYSELF?

_____

DATE:

I AM GRATEFUL FOR.....

1. _____
2. _____
3. _____
4. _____
5. _____

WHAT DO I APPRECIATE ABOUT MYSELF?

_____

✽ ✽ ✽ ✽ ✽

Sometimes we should express our gratitude for the small and simple things
-Joseph B. Worthlin

MY HEART IS FILLED WITH GRATITUDE
❀❀❀❀❀

DATE:

I AM GRATEFUL FOR.....
1. _____
2. _____
3. _____
4. _____
5. _____

WHAT DO I APPRECIATE ABOUT MYSELF?
_____

DATE:

I AM GRATEFUL FOR.....
1. _____
2. _____
3. _____
4. _____
5. _____

WHAT DO I APPRECIATE ABOUT MYSELF?
_____

We should certainly count our blessings, but we should also make our blessings count.

—Neal A. Maxwell

MY HEART IS FILLED WITH GRATITUDE
❀❀❀❀❀

DATE:

I AM GRATEFUL FOR.....
1. _____
2. _____
3. _____
4. _____
5. _____

WHAT DO I APPRECIATE ABOUT MYSELF?
_____

DATE:

I AM GRATEFUL FOR.....
1. _____
2. _____
3. _____
4. _____
5. _____

WHAT DO I APPRECIATE ABOUT MYSELF?
_____

Gratitude makes sense of our past, brings peace for today, and creates vision for tomorrow.

-Melody Beattie

MY HEART IS FILLED WITH GRATITUDE
❀❀❀❀❀

DATE:

I AM GRATEFUL FOR.....
1. _____
2. _____
3. _____
4. _____
5. _____

WHAT DO I APPRECIATE ABOUT MYSELF?
_____

DATE:

I AM GRATEFUL FOR.....
1. _____
2. _____
3. _____
4. _____
5. _____

WHAT DO I APPRECIATE ABOUT MYSELF?
_____

When you arise in the morning, think of what a precious priviledge it is to be alive - to breathe, to think, to enjoy, to love.

-Marcus Aurelius

MY HEART IS FILLED WITH GRATITUDE
❀❀❀❀

DATE:

I AM GRATEFUL FOR.....
1. _____
2. _____
3. _____
4. _____
5. _____

WHAT DO I APPRECIATE ABOUT MYSELF?
_____

DATE:

I AM GRATEFUL FOR.....
1. _____
2. _____
3. _____
4. _____
5. _____

WHAT DO I APPRECIATE ABOUT MYSELF?
_____

Acknowledging the good that you already have in your life is the foundation for all abundance.

- Eckhart Tolle

MY HEART IS FILLED WITH GRATITUDE
❀❀❀❀❀

DATE:

I AM GRATEFUL FOR.....
1. _____
2. _____
3. _____
4. _____
5. _____

WHAT DO I APPRECIATE ABOUT MYSELF?
_____

DATE:

I AM GRATEFUL FOR.....
1. _____
2. _____
3. _____
4. _____
5. _____

WHAT DO I APPRECIATE ABOUT MYSELF?
_____

❀❀❀❀❀

This is a wonderful day. I have never seen this one before.

-Maya Angelou

MY HEART IS FILLED WITH GRATITUDE
❋❋❋❋❋

DATE:

I AM GRATEFUL FOR.....
1. _____
2. _____
3. _____
4. _____
5. _____

WHAT DO I APPRECIATE ABOUT MYSELF?
_____

DATE:

I AM GRATEFUL FOR.....
1. _____
2. _____
3. _____
4. _____
5. _____

WHAT DO I APPRECIATE ABOUT MYSELF?
_____

He is a wise man who does not grieve for the things which he has not, but rejoices for those which he has.

-Epictetus

MY HEART IS FILLED WITH GRATITUDE

DATE:

I AM GRATEFUL FOR.....
1. _____
2. _____
3. _____
4. _____
5. _____

WHAT DO I APPRECIATE ABOUT MYSELF?
_____

DATE:

I AM GRATEFUL FOR.....
1. _____
2. _____
3. _____
4. _____
5. _____

WHAT DO I APPRECIATE ABOUT MYSELF?
_____

I like people who get excited about the change of seasons, the sound of the ocean, watching a sunset, the smell of rain & starry nights

—*Brooke Hampton*

MY HEART IS FILLED WITH GRATITUDE
❀❀❀❀❀

DATE:

I AM GRATEFUL FOR.....
1. _____
2. _____
3. _____
4. _____
5. _____

WHAT DO I APPRECIATE ABOUT MYSELF?
_____

DATE:

I AM GRATEFUL FOR.....
1. _____
2. _____
3. _____
4. _____
5. _____

WHAT DO I APPRECIATE ABOUT MYSELF?
_____

In life, one has a choice to take one or two paths: to wait for some special day or to celebrate each special day.
　　　　-Rasheed Ogunlaru

MY HEART IS FILLED WITH GRATITUDE
❋❋❋❋❋

DATE:

I AM GRATEFUL FOR.....
1. _____
2. _____
3. _____
4. _____
5. _____

WHAT DO I APPRECIATE ABOUT MYSELF?
_____

DATE:

I AM GRATEFUL FOR.....
1. _____
2. _____
3. _____
4. _____
5. _____

WHAT DO I APPRECIATE ABOUT MYSELF?
_____

❀❀❀❀❀

It is the sweet, simple things of life which are the real ones after all.

-Laura Ingalls Wilder

MY HEART IS FILLED WITH GRATITUDE
❀❀❀❀❀

DATE:

I AM GRATEFUL FOR.....
1. _____
2. _____
3. _____
4. _____
5. _____

WHAT DO I APPRECIATE ABOUT MYSELF?
_____

DATE:

I AM GRATEFUL FOR.....
1. _____
2. _____
3. _____
4. _____
5. _____

WHAT DO I APPRECIATE ABOUT MYSELF?
_____

The real gift of gratitude is that the more grateful you are, the more present you become.

- Robert Holden

MY HEART IS FILLED WITH GRATITUDE
❀❀❀❀❀

DATE:

I AM GRATEFUL FOR.....
1. _____
2. _____
3. _____
4. _____
5. _____

WHAT DO I APPRECIATE ABOUT MYSELF?
_____

DATE:

I AM GRATEFUL FOR.....
1. _____
2. _____
3. _____
4. _____
5. _____

WHAT DO I APPRECIATE ABOUT MYSELF?
_____

❋❋❋❋❋

The most simple things can bring the most happiness.

-Izabella Scorupco

MY HEART IS FILLED WITH GRATITUDE
❁ ❁ ❁ ❁ ❁

DATE:

I AM GRATEFUL FOR.....
1. _____
2. _____
3. _____
4. _____
5. _____

WHAT DO I APPRECIATE ABOUT MYSELF?
_____

DATE:

I AM GRATEFUL FOR.....
1. _____
2. _____
3. _____
4. _____
5. _____

WHAT DO I APPRECIATE ABOUT MYSELF?
_____

God gives us the gift of life; it is up to us to give ourselves the gift of living well.

-Voltaire

MY HEART IS FILLED WITH GRATITUDE
❀❀❀❀❀

DATE:

I AM GRATEFUL FOR.....

1. _____
2. _____
3. _____
4. _____
5. _____

WHAT DO I APPRECIATE ABOUT MYSELF?
_____

DATE:

I AM GRATEFUL FOR.....

1. _____
2. _____
3. _____
4. _____
5. _____

WHAT DO I APPRECIATE ABOUT MYSELF?
_____

The true secret of happiness lies in taking a genuine interest in all the details of daily life.

-William Morris

MY HEART IS FILLED WITH GRATITUDE
❀❀❀❀❀

DATE:

I AM GRATEFUL FOR.....
1. _____
2. _____
3. _____
4. _____
5. _____

WHAT DO I APPRECIATE ABOUT MYSELF?
_____

DATE:

I AM GRATEFUL FOR.....
1. _____
2. _____
3. _____
4. _____
5. _____

WHAT DO I APPRECIATE ABOUT MYSELF?
_____

Have kindness, empathy, and gratitude every single day.

-Jennifer Aniston

MY HEART IS FILLED WITH GRATITUDE
❀ ❀ ❀ ❀ ❀

DATE:

I AM GRATEFUL FOR.....
1. _____
2. _____
3. _____
4. _____
5. _____

WHAT DO I APPRECIATE ABOUT MYSELF?
_____

DATE:

I AM GRATEFUL FOR.....
1. _____
2. _____
3. _____
4. _____
5. _____

WHAT DO I APPRECIATE ABOUT MYSELF?
_____

Trade your expectation for appreciation and the world changes instantly.

- Tony Robbins

MY HEART IS FILLED WITH GRATITUDE
❀❀❀❀❀

DATE:

I AM GRATEFUL FOR.....
1. _____
2. _____
3. _____
4. _____
5. _____

WHAT DO I APPRECIATE ABOUT MYSELF?
_____

DATE:

I AM GRATEFUL FOR.....
1. _____
2. _____
3. _____
4. _____
5. _____

WHAT DO I APPRECIATE ABOUT MYSELF?
_____

When I started counting my blessings, my whole life turned around.

—Willie Nelson

MY HEART IS FILLED WITH GRATITUDE
❀❀❀❀❀

DATE:

I AM GRATEFUL FOR.....
1. _____
2. _____
3. _____
4. _____
5. _____

WHAT DO I APPRECIATE ABOUT MYSELF?
_____

DATE:

I AM GRATEFUL FOR.....
1. _____
2. _____
3. _____
4. _____
5. _____

WHAT DO I APPRECIATE ABOUT MYSELF?
_____

Shine brightly.
See beauty.
Love truly.
Give freely.
Create joyfully.
Live thankfully.

-Mary Davis

MY HEART IS FILLED WITH GRATITUDE
❃❃❃❃❃

DATE:

I AM GRATEFUL FOR.....
1. _____
2. _____
3. _____
4. _____
5. _____

WHAT DO I APPRECIATE ABOUT MYSELF?
_____

DATE:

I AM GRATEFUL FOR.....
1. _____
2. _____
3. _____
4. _____
5. _____

WHAT DO I APPRECIATE ABOUT MYSELF?
_____

That art of being happy lies in the power of extracting happiness from common things.

-Henry Ward Beecher

MY HEART IS FILLED WITH GRATITUDE
❀❀❀❀❀

DATE:

I AM GRATEFUL FOR.....
1. _____
2. _____
3. _____
4. _____
5. _____

WHAT DO I APPRECIATE ABOUT MYSELF?
_____

DATE:

I AM GRATEFUL FOR.....
1. _____
2. _____
3. _____
4. _____
5. _____

WHAT DO I APPRECIATE ABOUT MYSELF?
_____

Things turn out best for people who make the best of the way things turn out.

-John Wooden

MY HEART IS FILLED WITH GRATITUDE
❀❀❀❀❀

DATE:

I AM GRATEFUL FOR.....
1. _____
2. _____
3. _____
4. _____
5. _____

WHAT DO I APPRECIATE ABOUT MYSELF?
_____

DATE:

I AM GRATEFUL FOR.....
1. _____
2. _____
3. _____
4. _____
5. _____

WHAT DO I APPRECIATE ABOUT MYSELF?
_____

I always find beauty in things that are odd and imperfect- they are much more interesting.

-Marc Jacobs

MY HEART IS FILLED WITH GRATITUDE
❀❀❀❀❀

DATE:

I AM GRATEFUL FOR.....
1. _____
2. _____
3. _____
4. _____
5. _____

WHAT DO I APPRECIATE ABOUT MYSELF?
_____

DATE:

I AM GRATEFUL FOR.....
1. _____
2. _____
3. _____
4. _____
5. _____

WHAT DO I APPRECIATE ABOUT MYSELF?
_____

The most important thing is to enjoy your life - to be happy - it's all that matters.

-Audrey Hepburn

MY HEART IS FILLED WITH GRATITUDE
❀❀❀❀❀

DATE:

I AM GRATEFUL FOR.....
1. _____
2. _____
3. _____
4. _____
5. _____

WHAT DO I APPRECIATE ABOUT MYSELF?
_____

DATE:

I AM GRATEFUL FOR.....
1. _____
2. _____
3. _____
4. _____
5. _____

WHAT DO I APPRECIATE ABOUT MYSELF?
_____

I am happy because I'm grateful. I choose to be grateful. That gratitude allows me to be happy.
-Will Arnett

MY HEART IS FILLED WITH GRATITUDE
❀❀❀❀❀

DATE:

I AM GRATEFUL FOR.....
1. _____
2. _____
3. _____
4. _____
5. _____

WHAT DO I APPRECIATE ABOUT MYSELF?
_____

DATE:

I AM GRATEFUL FOR.....
1. _____
2. _____
3. _____
4. _____
5. _____

WHAT DO I APPRECIATE ABOUT MYSELF?
_____

Happines is not something you postpone for the future; it is something you design in the present.

-Jim Rohn

MY HEART IS FILLED WITH GRATITUDE
❀❀❀❀❀

DATE:

I AM GRATEFUL FOR.....

1. _____
2. _____
3. _____
4. _____
5. _____

WHAT DO I APPRECIATE ABOUT MYSELF?
_____

DATE:

I AM GRATEFUL FOR.....

1. _____
2. _____
3. _____
4. _____
5. _____

WHAT DO I APPRECIATE ABOUT MYSELF?
_____

❀❀❀❀❀

Some old fashion things like fresh air and sunshine are hard to beat.

-Laura Ingalls Wilder

MY HEART IS FILLED WITH GRATITUDE
❀❀❀❀❀

DATE:

I AM GRATEFUL FOR.....

1. _____
2. _____
3. _____
4. _____
5. _____

WHAT DO I APPRECIATE ABOUT MYSELF?
_____

DATE:

I AM GRATEFUL FOR.....

1. _____
2. _____
3. _____
4. _____
5. _____

WHAT DO I APPRECIATE ABOUT MYSELF?
_____

❀❀❀❀❀

If you are gracious, you have won the game.

- Stevie Nicks

MY HEART IS FILLED WITH GRATITUDE
❀❀❀❀❀

DATE:

I AM GRATEFUL FOR.....
1. _____
2. _____
3. _____
4. _____
5. _____

WHAT DO I APPRECIATE ABOUT MYSELF?
_____

DATE:

I AM GRATEFUL FOR.....
1. _____
2. _____
3. _____
4. _____
5. _____

WHAT DO I APPRECIATE ABOUT MYSELF?
_____

The more you praise and celebrate your life, the more there is in life to celebrate.

-Oprah Winfrey

MY HEART IS FILLED WITH GRATITUDE

DATE:

I AM GRATEFUL FOR.....
1. _____
2. _____
3. _____
4. _____
5. _____

WHAT DO I APPRECIATE ABOUT MYSELF?
_____

DATE:

I AM GRATEFUL FOR.....
1. _____
2. _____
3. _____
4. _____
5. _____

WHAT DO I APPRECIATE ABOUT MYSELF?
_____

If you want to find happiness, find gratitude.

– Steve Maraboli

MY HEART IS FILLED WITH GRATITUDE
❀❀❀❀❀

DATE:

I AM GRATEFUL FOR.....
1. _____
2. _____
3. _____
4. _____
5. _____

WHAT DO I APPRECIATE ABOUT MYSELF?
_____

DATE:

I AM GRATEFUL FOR.....
1. _____
2. _____
3. _____
4. _____
5. _____

WHAT DO I APPRECIATE ABOUT MYSELF?
_____

I don't have to chase extraordinary moments to find happiness - it's right in front of me if I'm paying attention and practicing gratitude.

-Brene Brown

MY HEART IS FILLED WITH GRATITUDE
❀❀❀❀❀

DATE:

I AM GRATEFUL FOR.....
1. _____
2. _____
3. _____
4. _____
5. _____

WHAT DO I APPRECIATE ABOUT MYSELF?
_____

DATE:

I AM GRATEFUL FOR.....
1. _____
2. _____
3. _____
4. _____
5. _____

WHAT DO I APPRECIATE ABOUT MYSELF?
_____

Gratitude helps you grow and expand; gratitude brings joy and laughter into your life and into the lives of all around you.

-Eileen Caddy

MY HEART IS FILLED WITH GRATITUDE
❀❀❀❀❀

DATE:

I AM GRATEFUL FOR.....
1. _____
2. _____
3. _____
4. _____
5. _____

WHAT DO I APPRECIATE ABOUT MYSELF?
_____

DATE:

I AM GRATEFUL FOR.....
1. _____
2. _____
3. _____
4. _____
5. _____

WHAT DO I APPRECIATE ABOUT MYSELF?
_____

Very little is needed to make a happy life; it is all within yourself, in your way of thinking.

-Marcus Aurelius

MY HEART IS FILLED WITH GRATITUDE

❀❀❀❀❀

DATE:

I AM GRATEFUL FOR.....

1. _____
2. _____
3. _____
4. _____
5. _____

WHAT DO I APPRECIATE ABOUT MYSELF?

_____

DATE:

I AM GRATEFUL FOR.....

1. _____
2. _____
3. _____
4. _____
5. _____

WHAT DO I APPRECIATE ABOUT MYSELF?

_____

The small happy moments add up. A little bit of joy goes a long way.

-Melissa McCarthy

MY HEART IS FILLED WITH GRATITUDE
❀❀❀❀❀

DATE:

I AM GRATEFUL FOR.....
1. _____
2. _____
3. _____
4. _____
5. _____

WHAT DO I APPRECIATE ABOUT MYSELF?
_____

DATE:

I AM GRATEFUL FOR.....
1. _____
2. _____
3. _____
4. _____
5. _____

WHAT DO I APPRECIATE ABOUT MYSELF?
_____

Put your heart, mind, and soul into even your smallest acts. This is the secret of success.

-Swami Sivananda

MY HEART IS FILLED WITH GRATITUDE
❈❈❈❈❈

DATE:

I AM GRATEFUL FOR.....
1. _____
2. _____
3. _____
4. _____
5. _____

WHAT DO I APPRECIATE ABOUT MYSELF?
_____

DATE:

I AM GRATEFUL FOR.....
1. _____
2. _____
3. _____
4. _____
5. _____

WHAT DO I APPRECIATE ABOUT MYSELF?
_____

Be thankful for what you have; you will end up having more. If you concentrate on what you don't have, you will never, ever have enough.

—*Oprah Winfrey*

MY HEART IS FILLED WITH GRATITUDE

DATE:

I AM GRATEFUL FOR.....
1.
2.
3.
4.
5.

WHAT DO I APPRECIATE ABOUT MYSELF?

DATE:

I AM GRATEFUL FOR.....
1.
2.
3.
4.
5.

WHAT DO I APPRECIATE ABOUT MYSELF?

❀❀❀❀❀

Enjoy the little things, for one day you may look back and realize they were the big things.

— Robert Brault

MY HEART IS FILLED WITH GRATITUDE
❀❀❀❀❀

DATE:

I AM GRATEFUL FOR.....
1. _____
2. _____
3. _____
4. _____
5. _____

WHAT DO I APPRECIATE ABOUT MYSELF?
_____

DATE:

I AM GRATEFUL FOR.....
1. _____
2. _____
3. _____
4. _____
5. _____

WHAT DO I APPRECIATE ABOUT MYSELF?
_____

Blessed are those who see beautiful things in humble places where other people see nothing.

— *Camile Pissarro*

MY HEART IS FILLED WITH GRATITUDE
❀❀❀❀❀

DATE:

I AM GRATEFUL FOR.....
1. _____
2. _____
3. _____
4. _____
5. _____

WHAT DO I APPRECIATE ABOUT MYSELF?
_____

DATE:

I AM GRATEFUL FOR.....
1. _____
2. _____
3. _____
4. _____
5. _____

WHAT DO I APPRECIATE ABOUT MYSELF?
_____

When we focus on our gratitude, the tide of disappointment goes out and the tide of love rushes in.

-Kristin Armstrong

MY HEART IS FILLED WITH GRATITUDE
❀❀❀❀

DATE:

I AM GRATEFUL FOR.....
1. _____
2. _____
3. _____
4. _____
5. _____

WHAT DO I APPRECIATE ABOUT MYSELF?
_____

DATE:

I AM GRATEFUL FOR.....
1. _____
2. _____
3. _____
4. _____
5. _____

WHAT DO I APPRECIATE ABOUT MYSELF?
_____

✿✿✿✿✿

Sometimes the smallest things take up the most room in your heart.

-Winnie the Pooh

MY HEART IS FILLED WITH GRATITUDE

DATE:

I AM GRATEFUL FOR.....
1. _____
2. _____
3. _____
4. _____
5. _____

WHAT DO I APPRECIATE ABOUT MYSELF?
_____

DATE:

I AM GRATEFUL FOR.....
1. _____
2. _____
3. _____
4. _____
5. _____

WHAT DO I APPRECIATE ABOUT MYSELF?
_____

When you are grateful - when you can see what you have - you unlock blessings to flow in your life.

-*Suze Orman*

MY HEART IS FILLED WITH GRATITUDE
❀❀❀❀❀

DATE:

I AM GRATEFUL FOR.....
1._____
2._____
3._____
4._____
5._____

WHAT DO I APPRECIATE ABOUT MYSELF?
_____

DATE:

I AM GRATEFUL FOR.....
1._____
2._____
3._____
4._____
5._____

WHAT DO I APPRECIATE ABOUT MYSELF?
_____

❋❋❋❋❋

Gratitude and attitude are not challenges; they are choices.

- Robert Braathe

MY HEART IS FILLED WITH GRATITUDE
❀❀❀❀❀

DATE:

I AM GRATEFUL FOR.....
1. _____
2. _____
3. _____
4. _____
5. _____

WHAT DO I APPRECIATE ABOUT MYSELF?
_____

DATE:

I AM GRATEFUL FOR.....
1. _____
2. _____
3. _____
4. _____
5. _____

WHAT DO I APPRECIATE ABOUT MYSELF?
_____

❋❋❋❋❋

Through the eyes of gratitude, everything is a miracle.

-Mary Davis

MY HEART IS FILLED WITH GRATITUDE
❀❀❀❀❀

DATE:

I AM GRATEFUL FOR.....
1. _____
2. _____
3. _____
4. _____
5. _____

WHAT DO I APPRECIATE ABOUT MYSELF?
_____

DATE:

I AM GRATEFUL FOR.....
1. _____
2. _____
3. _____
4. _____
5. _____

WHAT DO I APPRECIATE ABOUT MYSELF?
_____

Gratitude can transform common days into thanksgiving, turn routine jobs into joy, and change ordinary opportunities into blessings.
—William Arthur Ward

MY HEART IS FILLED WITH GRATITUDE
❀❀❀❀❀

DATE:

I AM GRATEFUL FOR.....
1. _____
2. _____
3. _____
4. _____
5. _____

WHAT DO I APPRECIATE ABOUT MYSELF?
_____

DATE:

I AM GRATEFUL FOR.....
1. _____
2. _____
3. _____
4. _____
5. _____

WHAT DO I APPRECIATE ABOUT MYSELF?
_____

✿✿✿✿✿

Gratitude is the fairest blossom which springs from the soul.

-Henry Ward Beecher

MY HEART IS FILLED WITH GRATITUDE

DATE:

I AM GRATEFUL FOR.....
1. _____
2. _____
3. _____
4. _____
5. _____

WHAT DO I APPRECIATE ABOUT MYSELF?
_____

DATE:

I AM GRATEFUL FOR.....
1. _____
2. _____
3. _____
4. _____
5. _____

WHAT DO I APPRECIATE ABOUT MYSELF?
_____

✿✿✿✿✿

We often take for granted the very things that most deserve our gratitude.

— Cynthia Ozick

MY HEART IS FILLED WITH GRATITUDE
❀❀❀❀❀

DATE: _____

I AM GRATEFUL FOR.....
1. _____
2. _____
3. _____
4. _____
5. _____

WHAT DO I APPRECIATE ABOUT MYSELF?
_____

DATE: _____

I AM GRATEFUL FOR.....
1. _____
2. _____
3. _____
4. _____
5. _____

WHAT DO I APPRECIATE ABOUT MYSELF?
_____

You cannot do kindness too soon because you never know how soon it will be to late.

-Ralph Waldo Emerson

MY HEART IS FILLED WITH GRATITUDE
❀❀❀❀❀

DATE:

I AM GRATEFUL FOR.....
1. _____
2. _____
3. _____
4. _____
5. _____

WHAT DO I APPRECIATE ABOUT MYSELF?
_____

DATE:

I AM GRATEFUL FOR.....
1. _____
2. _____
3. _____
4. _____
5. _____

WHAT DO I APPRECIATE ABOUT MYSELF?
_____

I would maintain that thanks are the highest form of thought, and that gratitude is happiness doubled by wonder.

-Gilbert C. Chesterton

MY HEART IS FILLED WITH GRATITUDE

❀❀❀❀❀

DATE:

I AM GRATEFUL FOR.....
1. _____
2. _____
3. _____
4. _____
5. _____

WHAT DO I APPRECIATE ABOUT MYSELF?
_____

DATE:

I AM GRATEFUL FOR.....
1. _____
2. _____
3. _____
4. _____
5. _____

WHAT DO I APPRECIATE ABOUT MYSELF?
_____

Gratitude will shift you to a higher frequency, and you will attract much better things.

—*Rhonda Byrne*

MY HEART IS FILLED WITH GRATITUDE

DATE:

I AM GRATEFUL FOR.....
1. _____
2. _____
3. _____
4. _____
5. _____

WHAT DO I APPRECIATE ABOUT MYSELF?
_____

DATE:

I AM GRATEFUL FOR.....
1. _____
2. _____
3. _____
4. _____
5. _____

WHAT DO I APPRECIATE ABOUT MYSELF?
_____

Two kinds of gratitude: The sudden kind we feel for what we take; the larger kind we feel for what we give.

-Edwin Arlington Robinson

MY HEART IS FILLED WITH GRATITUDE
❊❊❊❊❊

DATE:

I AM GRATEFUL FOR.....
1. _____
2. _____
3. _____
4. _____
5. _____

WHAT DO I APPRECIATE ABOUT MYSELF?
_____

DATE:

I AM GRATEFUL FOR.....
1. _____
2. _____
3. _____
4. _____
5. _____

WHAT DO I APPRECIATE ABOUT MYSELF?
_____

❋❋❋❋❋

The more grateful I am, the more beauty I see.

-Mary Davis

MY HEART IS FILLED WITH GRATITUDE
❀❀❀❀❀

DATE:

I AM GRATEFUL FOR.....
1. _____
2. _____
3. _____
4. _____
5. _____

WHAT DO I APPRECIATE ABOUT MYSELF?
_____

DATE:

I AM GRATEFUL FOR.....
1. _____
2. _____
3. _____
4. _____
5. _____

WHAT DO I APPRECIATE ABOUT MYSELF?
_____

Some people grumble that roses have thorns; I am grateful that thorns have roses.

-Alphonse Karr

MY HEART IS FILLED WITH GRATITUDE

❀❀❀❀❀

DATE:

I AM GRATEFUL FOR.....
1. _____
2. _____
3. _____
4. _____
5. _____

WHAT DO I APPRECIATE ABOUT MYSELF?
_____

DATE:

I AM GRATEFUL FOR.....
1. _____
2. _____
3. _____
4. _____
5. _____

WHAT DO I APPRECIATE ABOUT MYSELF?
_____

There is a calmness to a life lived in gratitude, a quiet joy.

-Ralph H. Blum

MY HEART IS FILLED WITH GRATITUDE
❀❀❀❀❀

DATE:

I AM GRATEFUL FOR.....
1. _____
2. _____
3. _____
4. _____
5. _____

WHAT DO I APPRECIATE ABOUT MYSELF?
_____

DATE:

I AM GRATEFUL FOR.....
1. _____
2. _____
3. _____
4. _____
5. _____

WHAT DO I APPRECIATE ABOUT MYSELF?
_____

❀❀❀❀❀

The root of joy is gratefulness.

-David Steindl-Rast

MY HEART IS FILLED WITH GRATITUDE
❀❀❀❀❀

DATE:

I AM GRATEFUL FOR.....
1. _____
2. _____
3. _____
4. _____
5. _____

WHAT DO I APPRECIATE ABOUT MYSELF?
_____

DATE:

I AM GRATEFUL FOR.....
1. _____
2. _____
3. _____
4. _____
5. _____

WHAT DO I APPRECIATE ABOUT MYSELF?
_____

As we express our gratitude, we must never forget that the highest appreciation is not to utter words, but to live by them.

-John F. Kennedy

MY HEART IS FILLED WITH GRATITUDE
❀❀❀❀❀

DATE:

I AM GRATEFUL FOR.....
1. _____
2. _____
3. _____
4. _____
5. _____

WHAT DO I APPRECIATE ABOUT MYSELF?
_____

DATE:

I AM GRATEFUL FOR.....
1. _____
2. _____
3. _____
4. _____
5. _____

WHAT DO I APPRECIATE ABOUT MYSELF?
_____

Gratitude for the present moment and the fullness of life now is the true prosperity.

- Eckhart Tolle

MY HEART IS FILLED WITH GRATITUDE
❀❀❀❀❀

DATE:

I AM GRATEFUL FOR.....
1. _____
2. _____
3. _____
4. _____
5. _____

WHAT DO I APPRECIATE ABOUT MYSELF?
_____

DATE:

I AM GRATEFUL FOR.....
1. _____
2. _____
3. _____
4. _____
5. _____

WHAT DO I APPRECIATE ABOUT MYSELF?
_____

Strive to find things to be thankful for, and just look for the good in who you are .

-Bethany Hamilton

MY HEART IS FILLED WITH GRATITUDE
❀❀❀❀❀

DATE:

I AM GRATEFUL FOR.....

1. _____
2. _____
3. _____
4. _____
5. _____

WHAT DO I APPRECIATE ABOUT MYSELF?
_____

DATE:

I AM GRATEFUL FOR.....

1. _____
2. _____
3. _____
4. _____
5. _____

WHAT DO I APPRECIATE ABOUT MYSELF?
_____

✹✹✹✹✹

When you are grateful, fear disappears and abundance appears.

-Anthony Robbins

MY HEART IS FILLED WITH GRATITUDE
❀❀❀❀❀

DATE:

I AM GRATEFUL FOR.....
1. _____
2. _____
3. _____
4. _____
5. _____

WHAT DO I APPRECIATE ABOUT MYSELF?
_____

DATE:

I AM GRATEFUL FOR.....
1. _____
2. _____
3. _____
4. _____
5. _____

WHAT DO I APPRECIATE ABOUT MYSELF?
_____

When it comes to life the critical thing is whether you take things for granted or take them with gratitude.

-G. K. Chesterton

MY HEART IS FILLED WITH GRATITUDE
❀❀❀❀❀

DATE:

I AM GRATEFUL FOR.....
1. _____
2. _____
3. _____
4. _____
5. _____

WHAT DO I APPRECIATE ABOUT MYSELF?
_____

DATE:

I AM GRATEFUL FOR.....
1. _____
2. _____
3. _____
4. _____
5. _____

WHAT DO I APPRECIATE ABOUT MYSELF?
_____

❀❀❀❀❀

Feeling gratitude and not expressing it is like wrapping a present and not giving it.

-William Arthur Ward

MY HEART IS FILLED WITH GRATITUDE
❀❀❀❀

DATE:

I AM GRATEFUL FOR.....

1. _____
2. _____
3. _____
4. _____
5. _____

WHAT DO I APPRECIATE ABOUT MYSELF?
_____

DATE:

I AM GRATEFUL FOR.....

1. _____
2. _____
3. _____
4. _____
5. _____

WHAT DO I APPRECIATE ABOUT MYSELF?
_____

✿✿✿✿✿

Gratitude is the most exquisite form of courtesy.

-Jacques Maritian

MY HEART IS FILLED WITH GRATITUDE
❀❀❀❀❀

DATE:

I AM GRATEFUL FOR.....
1. _____
2. _____
3. _____
4. _____
5. _____

WHAT DO I APPRECIATE ABOUT MYSELF?
_____

DATE:

I AM GRATEFUL FOR.....
1. _____
2. _____
3. _____
4. _____
5. _____

WHAT DO I APPRECIATE ABOUT MYSELF?
_____

Learn to be thankful for what you have while you pursue all that you want.

-Jim Rohn

MY HEART IS FILLED WITH GRATITUDE
❀❀❀❀❀

DATE:

I AM GRATEFUL FOR.....
1. _____
2. _____
3. _____
4. _____
5. _____

WHAT DO I APPRECIATE ABOUT MYSELF?
_____

DATE:

I AM GRATEFUL FOR.....
1. _____
2. _____
3. _____
4. _____
5. _____

WHAT DO I APPRECIATE ABOUT MYSELF?
_____

The way to develop the best that is in a person is by appreciation and encouragement.

- Charles Schwab

MY HEART IS FILLED WITH GRATITUDE
❀❀❀❀❀

DATE:

I AM GRATEFUL FOR.....
1. _____
2. _____
3. _____
4. _____
5. _____

WHAT DO I APPRECIATE ABOUT MYSELF?
_____

DATE:

I AM GRATEFUL FOR.....
1. _____
2. _____
3. _____
4. _____
5. _____

WHAT DO I APPRECIATE ABOUT MYSELF?
_____

❀❀❀❀❀

The roots to all goodness lie in the soil of appreciation for goodness.

-Dalai Lama

MY HEART IS FILLED WITH GRATITUDE
❀❀❀❀❀

DATE:

I AM GRATEFUL FOR.....
1. _____
2. _____
3. _____
4. _____
5. _____

WHAT DO I APPRECIATE ABOUT MYSELF?
_____

DATE:

I AM GRATEFUL FOR.....
1. _____
2. _____
3. _____
4. _____
5. _____

WHAT DO I APPRECIATE ABOUT MYSELF?
_____

There are only two ways to live your life. One is as though nothing is a miracle. The other is as though everything is a miracle.

—Albert Einstein

MY HEART IS FILLED WITH GRATITUDE
❀❀❀❀❀

DATE:

I AM GRATEFUL FOR.....
1. _____
2. _____
3. _____
4. _____
5. _____

WHAT DO I APPRECIATE ABOUT MYSELF?
_____

DATE:

I AM GRATEFUL FOR.....
1. _____
2. _____
3. _____
4. _____
5. _____

WHAT DO I APPRECIATE ABOUT MYSELF?
_____

If you want to find happiness, find gratitude.

- Steve Marabloi

MY HEART IS FILLED WITH GRATITUDE

❀❀❀❀❀

DATE:

I AM GRATEFUL FOR.....

1. _____
2. _____
3. _____
4. _____
5. _____

WHAT DO I APPRECIATE ABOUT MYSELF?
_____

DATE:

I AM GRATEFUL FOR.....

1. _____
2. _____
3. _____
4. _____
5. _____

WHAT DO I APPRECIATE ABOUT MYSELF?
_____

Be Mindful.
Be Grateful.
Be Positive.
Be True.
Be Kind.

-Roy T. Bennett

MY HEART IS FILLED WITH GRATITUDE
❀❀❀❀❀

DATE:

I AM GRATEFUL FOR.....
1. _____
2. _____
3. _____
4. _____
5. _____

WHAT DO I APPRECIATE ABOUT MYSELF?
_____

DATE:

I AM GRATEFUL FOR.....
1. _____
2. _____
3. _____
4. _____
5. _____

WHAT DO I APPRECIATE ABOUT MYSELF?
_____

Start where you are. Use what you have. Do what you can.

- Aurthur Ashe

MY HEART IS FILLED WITH GRATITUDE
❀❀❀❀❀

DATE:

I AM GRATEFUL FOR.....

1. _____
2. _____
3. _____
4. _____
5. _____

WHAT DO I APPRECIATE ABOUT MYSELF?
_____

DATE:

I AM GRATEFUL FOR.....

1. _____
2. _____
3. _____
4. _____
5. _____

WHAT DO I APPRECIATE ABOUT MYSELF?
_____

THANK YOU!

Reflect

Reflect

Reflect

Reflect

Reflect

Reflect

Reflect

Reflect